CHOCOLATE!

CHOCOLATE!

CHOCOLATE
The Consuming Passion

by Sandra Boynton

WORKMAN PUBLISHING ★ NEW YORK

FOR MY ABSOLUTELY TERRIFIC CHILDREN—
CAITLIN McEWAN, KEITH BOYNTON,
DEVIN McEWAN, and DARCY BOYNTON

CHOCOLATE: The Consuming Passion

Copyright ©1982, 2015 Sandra Boynton
All rights reserved. No portion of this book may be reproduced—mechanically,
electronically, or by any other means, including photocopying—without written permission
of the publisher and author.
Published simultaneously in Canada by Thomas Allen & Son Ltd.
Library of Congress Cataloging-in-Publication data is available.
ISBN 978-0-7611-8563-5

p. 1 ornate frame adapted from a posting by Moxylyn, deviantart.com
p. 36 shell plant production sequence text from Chocolate, Cocoa and Confectionery by Bernard W. Minifie,
The AVI Publishing Co., Westport, CT, 1980
p. 44 quotation from the 2008 Journal of Indian Society of Pedodontics and Preventive Dentistry

WORKMAN PUBLISHING COMPANY, INC.
225 Varick Street, New York, NY 10014-4381
WORKMAN is a registered trademark of Workman Publishing Co., Inc.
Manufactured in China   NEW EDITION First Printing September 2015
10 9 8 7 6 5 4 3 2 1

ACKNOWLEDGMENTS

There are many without whom this book
would have been impossible.

There are some others without whom
it would have been a heck of a lot easier.

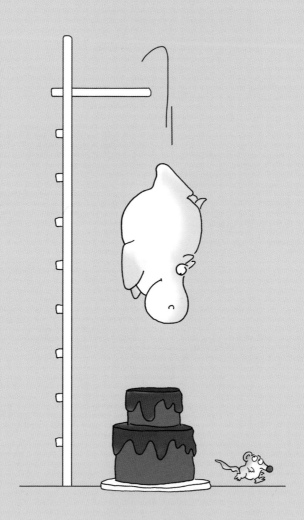

C CONTENTS

The Mayans and Aztecs made from the beans of the cacao tree a hot drink that they called *xocoatl* (shock-WA-tull). The conquering Spanish returned home with *chocolate* (chō-cō-LAH-tay) in 1528. A royal wedding in 1615 brought the drink to France, where they called it *chocolat* (shō-cō-LAH). In time, the wondrous elixir crossed the Channel, and the English welcomed the *chocolata* (Stubbes, 1662), *jocolatte* (Pepys, 1664), *jacolatte* (Evelyn, 1682), and *chockelet* (Evelyn again, 1684).

In fact, it was not until chocolate came to the United States that people began spelling and pronouncing it correctly: **CHOCOLATE**.

CHOCK-lit.

THE CHOCOLATE ELITE

Research tells us that fourteen out of any ten individuals like chocolate. But what is "liking chocolate"? There are, of course, infinite degrees of "like."

DEGREES OF LIKE
(a dramatization)

Q: Do you like chocolate?

And what is really meant by "chocolate"? It could refer to **CHOCOLATE,** or perhaps **chocolate.** Then there's **CHOCOLATE,** *chocolate,* **CHOCOLATE,** *Chocolates,* and EVIL SYNTHETIC CHOCOLATE.

Or we may find among these chocolate-likers those who favor chocolate food experience over chocolate candy—things such as chocolate cream pies, ginger brownies, chocolate chip cookies, chocolate mint soufflés, chocolate-covered graham crackers, chocolate malts, pinwheels, chocolate bagels, chocolate peppermint ice cream, chocolate peanut butter nutballs, chocolate nib nutballs, chocolate gelato, chocolate croissants, chocolate turtles, chocolate hot chocolate danish, chocolate crackers, chocolate custard, chocolate orange fizz, chocolate malted milk, chocolate chip salad, chocolate marzipan, chocolate molé, chocolate potato, chocolate cheese, chocolate layer cake, cocoa quiche, chocolate bavarian, chocolate surprise cookies, chocolate pavé, chocolate omelets, chocolate crackers, chocolate caramel danish, hot fudge sundaes, chocolate crackers, chocolate fritters, chocolate cinnamon chocolate eggplant casserole, chocolate cream mocha tortes, chocolate meringues, chocolate malt frappes, chocolate raspberry mango milk, chocolate plum pudding, chocolate chunk shortbread, chocolate cucumber chocolate burnt sugar doughnuts, chocolate chili gum, chocolate banana cake, crème de cacao, chocolate pretzels, to name a few.

Certainly this book is not for everyone who merely claims to "like chocolate." It will serve little purpose for those who would just as soon have _____ as chocolate.
<small>ANY NOUN</small>

Rather, this book was written for the Chocolate Elite—

those select billions who like chocolate in all its glorious and infinite variety, using "like" as in "I like to breathe."

The true connoisseur shuns all chocolate novelty in favor of the uncompromised bittersweet experience. This is the *gourmet*.

At the other extreme is the individual who will embrace chocolate in any form: the *gourmand*.

And right in the middle of the field is she who is partial always to the gentleness and variety of milk chocolate: the *gourmoo*.

Part One

THE MANY FACES OF CHOCOLATE

CHOCOLATE PROFILE № 1

The Pastoral Chocolatist

PERSONALITY	THOUGHTFUL, TIMID
LIKES	SPRINGTIME
DISLIKES	YODELERS
FAVORITE PASTIME	RUMINATING

CHOCOLATE of CHOICE: Milk Chocolate

ABOUT
MILK CHOCOLATE

Milk chocolate has long been the most popular kind of chocolate for eating and general hoarding purposes. It is made from **chocolate liquor** (the centers of cacao beans—the "nibs"— ground to a liquid) plus sugar, milk solids, cocoa butter, and vanilla. The finished chocolate usually comes in bars, though there are also many perky novelty shapes such as chocolate rabbits,

chocolate eggs,

chocolate model airplane kits,

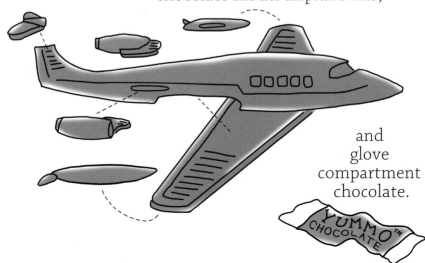

and glove compartment chocolate.

In many "fun" forms of milk chocolate, the quality of the chocolate itself may be disappointing, for the simple reason that the manufacturer considers the *shape* of the chocolate, not the taste, to be the primary lure. (Although honestly, the shapes are not always that appealing either.)

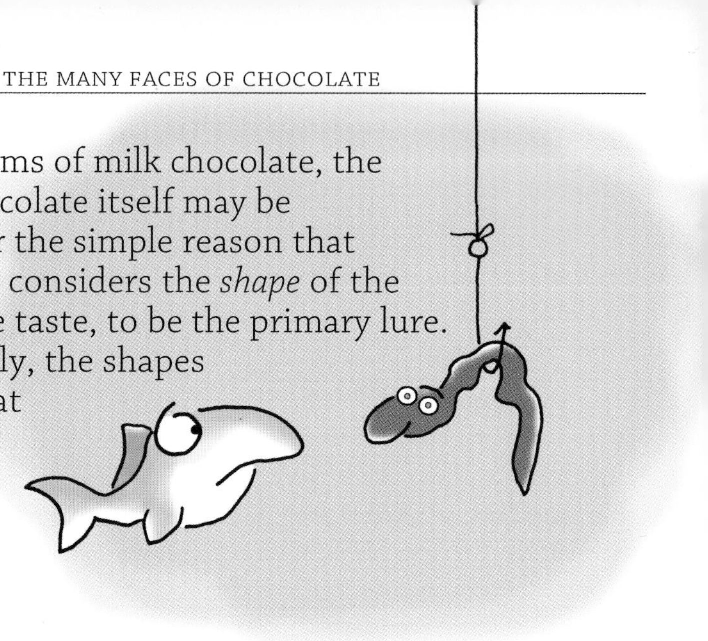

And even when the chocolate is good, there may, alas, not be very much of it. Since most molded chocolate is hollow, the impression of quantity is frequently a cruel illusion.

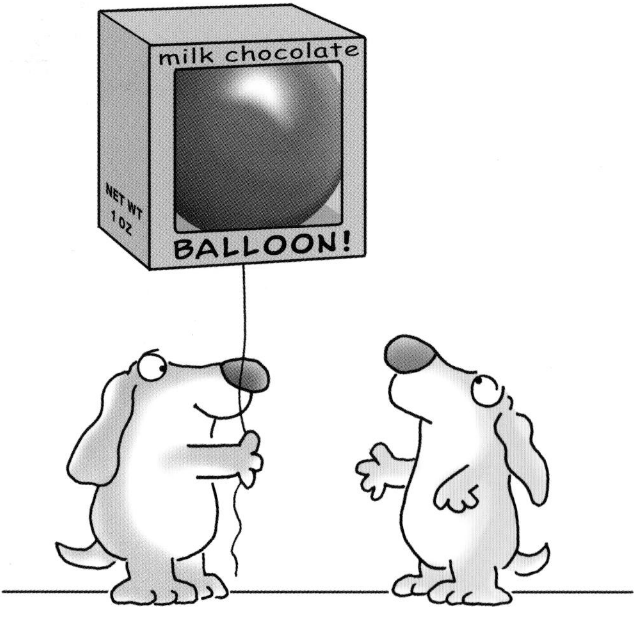
milk chocolate
NET WT
1 OZ
BALLOON!

For hard-core enjoyment, it may be wisest to stay with the standard solid milk chocolate bar—available in many sizes, ranging from bite-size miniatures to convenient purse-size bars to edible commercial furnishings.

Milk Chocolate Bar (industrial size)

Beyond the astonishing range of milk chocolate shapes and sizes, there is also a staggering variety of combination candy. A versatile crowd-pleaser, milk chocolate can be found happily encasing savory peanut butter, sumptuous caramel, sun-sweetened raisins, delicate marshmallow, crispy rice, luscious roasted almonds, you name it.

Cynics, of course, do not appreciate milk chocolate. Such is the price of widespread popularity.

THE BIRTH OF MILK CHOCOLATE

Although "drinking chocolate" was a well-established indulgence in Europe by the second half of the nineteenth century, "eating chocolate"—introduced by Fry & Sons in 1847—was still something of a novelty.

Daniel Peter, renowned Swiss chocolatier, had the inspired idea to look for some other ingredient that he could combine with chocolate to smooth out its texture and balance its rough flavor. "What does Switzerland have in abundance," he wondered, "that I could use to process with the chocolate?" His answer: Cheese. The resulting experiment was notoriously unsuccessful.

A number of ill-fated mixtures (grass, edelweiss, watch movements, numbered bank accounts) followed. In fact, no one really knows how—in 1874—Peter finally stumbled on the answer, although there is some evidence that the simple suggestion of a neighbor ("Moo.") was the crucial catalyst.

Daniel Peter

Unidentified Collaborator

CHOCOLATE PROFILE № 2
The Thoughtful Theobromian

PERSONALITY	AFFABLE, SKEPTICAL
LIKES	LIVE THEATER
DISLIKES	LIVE THEATER
FAVORITE PASTIME	SPELUNKING

CHOCOLATE of CHOICE: Dark Chocolate

ABOUT
DARK CHOCOLATE

"Dark chocolate" can mean many wildly different things, depending especially on the percentage of the bitter chocolate liquor. This can be anywhere from 15 percent to 99 percent, with the remainder being mostly sugar. The higher the percentage of the liquor, the less sweet the chocolate.

Chocolate at the milder end of the dark spectrum is usually called **semisweet chocolate**, and is basically milk chocolate without the milk. Yet the terminology is quite variable. There is no technical distinction between a chocolate that is labeled "semisweet" and one that is called "sweet" or "bittersweet" or "hemi-demi-semisweet," which isn't a thing. Yet. Unfortunately, the terminology is bound to remain a mystery to consumers, since chocolate executives are unwilling to disclose the complex methods by which they determine how they will label a given dark chocolate bar.

In contrast to the darker darks (also known as "high-cacao" bars), semisweet is a nicely uncomplicated chocolate, a pleasant companion on a quiet afternoon.

It also is a valued dessert ingredient—for soufflés, mousses, puddings, and cakes. And semisweet shavings grace many a fancy torte.

Among all of semisweet chocolate's contributions to the universe, surely the most noteworthy is the chocolate chip. The chips were first manufactured by the Nestlé Company, specifically for use in innkeeper Ruth Wakefield's inspired 1930s invention, "Toll House Chocolate Crunch Cookies." The cookies are still the most common vehicle for these famous morsels, although chocolate chips continue to inspire many other creative uses as well.

HIGH STAKES POKER

In place of the usual clay, ceramic, or plastic poker chips, try using premium semisweet chocolate chips. This game requires considerably more control of the facial muscles than ordinary poker: With one impetuous move, you could wipe out your entire winnings, even while holding a royal flush.

Farther along the dark chocolate spectrum is **bittersweet chocolate**, which is usually around half chocolate liquor and half sugar. You may also find chocolate labeled as "Extra Dark" or "Extra Bittersweet," to differentiate it from the gentler darks. These bars usually contain upwards of 65 percent cacao by weight. Some makers helpfully display their bar's cacao percentage right on the front of the pretentious wrapper.

If you are heading in this intense very-high-cacao-chocolate direction, you may find it worthwhile to develop a taste for **bitter chocolate**, which is completely unsweetened. Here you will find the most health benefits. Equally important, bitter chocolate has this marked advantage over all other kinds of chocolate: Pretty much no one will ask more than once to share it with you.

ON ICE CREAM

A surprising number of dark chocolate aficionados actually prefer vanilla ice cream to chocolate ice cream. This fact is not widely known because these individuals do not readily admit to this seemingly déclassé preference.

Overall, vanilla ice cream accounts for more than thirty percent of all ice cream sales, compared to a measly nine percent for chocolate ice cream. Careless statisticians conclude that "vanilla is a more popular flavoring than chocolate." Hardly. It would be far more logical to observe that the chocolate statement made by ice cream must not be particularly persuasive.

CHOCOLATE!

You must be joking.

CHOCOLATE PROFILE №3

That Vanilla Guy

PERSONALITY	CONFIDENTLY BLAND
LIKES	TALKING REALLY LOUDLY
DISLIKES	BOOKS
FAVORITE PASTIME	CAROB-BEAN CRUISES

CHOCOLATE of CHOICE: White Chocolate

ABOUT
WHITE CHOCOLATE

There is some disagreement as to whether white chocolate is in fact "real" chocolate. Its ingredients—cocoa butter, sugar, milk solids, vanilla—are largely the same as those in milk chocolate, but without the cocoa solids portion of the chocolate liquor.

Anyone who claims that the absence of cocoa disqualifies white chocolate as chocolate is quibbling. The same purist would probably argue that water and fructose is not "real" wine.

White chocolate has great appeal for those who find that color and flavor interfere with the experience of texture.

How do you tell a really good white chocolate from a so-so white chocolate? Your senses, such as they are, will guide you. The very best white chocolate will have an understated color, like this:

It has a subtle, pulpy fragrance, like this:

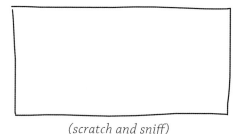

(scratch and sniff)

And it tastes like this:

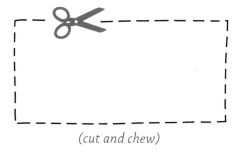

(cut and chew)

A NOTE ON CAROB

Carob is a brown powder created from the dried pulverized fruit of a Mediterranean evergreen. Some consider carob to be a reasonable substitute for chocolate because it has some similar nutrients (calcium, phosphorus) and because it can—when combined with vegetable fat and sugar—be made to approximate the color and consistency of chocolate. Of course, the same arguments can also be made in favor of dirt.

If you are eager to learn more about carob and the many other imitation chocolate products that are on the market, I really don't know what to tell you.

AN CHOCOLATES★DAN'S CHOCOLATES★E.H.CHOCOLATIER★ELIZABET
★FRAN'S CHOCOLATES★FRANÇOIS PAYARD★FRENCH BROAD CHOCOL
BOR SWEETS★HUDSON VALLEY CHOCOLATES★JACQUES TORRES CHOC
N-PAUL HÉVIN★JOHN KELLY CHOCOLATES★KAILUA CANDY COMPANY
COLATES★L'AMOURETTE★L.A.BURDICK CHOCOLATES★LA MAISON DU
T★LAKE CHAMPLAIN CHOCOLATES★LAURENT GERBAUD★LEONIDAS★I
OLATES★MAX BRENNER★MY SWEET BRIGADEIRO★NEUHAUS★NOI SIR
C CHOCOLATE★NORMAN LOVE CONFECTIONS★PADOVANI'S CHOCOLAT
ROGER★PIERRE HERMÉ★PIERRE MARCOLINI★PIERRE VIVIER CHOCO
DOLCE★RECCHIUTI CONFECTIONS★RICHARD DONNELLY FINE CHOCO
CHART★SARATOGA CHOCOLATES★SEE'S CANDIES★SUZANNE'S CHOCO

CHOCOLATE PROFILE № 4

The Sensuous Chocophile

PERSONALITY	MOODY, IMPULSIVE
LIKES	VISITORS
DISLIKES	CAMPING TRIPS
FAVORITE PASTIME	BUBBLE BATHS

CHOCOLATE of CHOICE: Chocolates

TEUSCHER CHOCOLATES OF SWITZERLAND★VALERIE CONFECTIONS★ECTIONS★
COLATES★VOSGES HAUT-CHOCOLAT★WITTAMER★WOODHOUSE CHOCO
DLATTI★BENDICKS OF MAYFAIR★BERNACHON★CHAPON★CHOCOLATE
CALLEBAUT★CHRISTOPHER ELBOW ARTISANAL CHOCOLATES★CHRIS
AN CHOCOLATES★DAN'S CHOCOLATES★E.H.CHOCOLATIER★ELIZABET
★FRAN'S CHOCOLATES★FRANÇOIS PAYARD★FRENCH BROAD CHOCOL
BOR SWEETS★HUDSON VALLEY CHOCOLATES★JACQUES TORRES CHOC
N-PAUL HÉVIN★JOHN KELLY CHOCOLATES★KAILUA CANDY COMPANY
COLATES★L'AMOURETTE★L.A.BURDICK CHOCOLATES★LA MAISON DU
T★LAKE CHAMPLAIN CHOCOLATES★LAURENT GERBAUD★LEONIDAS★
OLATES★MAX BRENNER★MY SWEET BRIGADEIRO★NEUHAUS★NOI

CREAMS *AND* VARIATIONS

Whoever said, "The best things in life are free," was, of course, just kidding. The best things go for upwards of $65.00 a pound.

Chocolates refers to any assortment of bite-size, chocolate-covered, overpriced candies. Most chocolates are given as gifts—for birthdays or anniversaries, as gestures of sincere appreciation or gratitude or manipulation, and especially to spark romance.

A gift of fine chocolates can be an eloquent expression of a lover's true passion.

Usually, chocolates come preselected in decorative cardboard boxes or tins, though many shops that specialize in chocolates will allow you to assemble your own assortment piece by piece.

In theory, the advantage of choosing your own is that you know what you are getting. Yet buyers are often as baffled by labeled chocolates as by mystery assortments. Too ashamed to admit ignorance, these unfortunate individuals are doomed to an endless procession of the familiar—caramels, nuts, creams.

One chocolate with an elusive definition is the **cordial**. Most chocolates consumers are unclear as to whether the term "cordial" means that the filling is alcoholic. There are two basic answers to this:

And any chocolates enthusiast should know that **truffles** are the finest chocolates possible. Nevertheless, there are those who shun truffles out of sheer ignorance. A chocolate truffle is *not* made with a rare edible potato-shaped fungus that grows underground. It is fancifully called "truffle" because it looks something like a regular old truffle; and because it, too, is a delicacy; and because it is hunted down in much the same way as its fungal counterpart.

Sniffing out truffles

This still does not explain what exactly a chocolate truffle *is*. It has something to do with heavy cream and superb bittersweet chocolate and frenetic whipping. All good. If you need a more precise defintion, it may be best to ask an expert.

HOW CHOCOLATES ARE MADE

There are four principal methods used to cover things with chocolate. Depending on the sophistication of their target market, makers chocolate-coat centers that range from superb freshly-made micro-batch confectionery to whatever that stuff is inside of malt balls.

1. *Enrobing* This is the most common coating method. A conveyor belt carries the centers through a machine that showers them with warm liquid chocolate.

2. *Panning* In this case, chocolate is sprayed onto the centers as they rotate in revolving pans; then cool air is blown into the pans to harden the coating. This technique is used largely for manufacturing inexpensive candy. Panning is great for coating truckloads of durable centers, such as raisins or peanuts (after first removing the trucks).

3. *Dipping* This method involves the quick immersion of candy centers in a large vessel of molten chocolate. The chocolate used here is usually **couverture**—a premium blend of cacao, sugar, and extra cocoa butter. Since dipping is most often done by hand, this labor-intensive process is generally used only by small producers of high-end boutique chocolates.

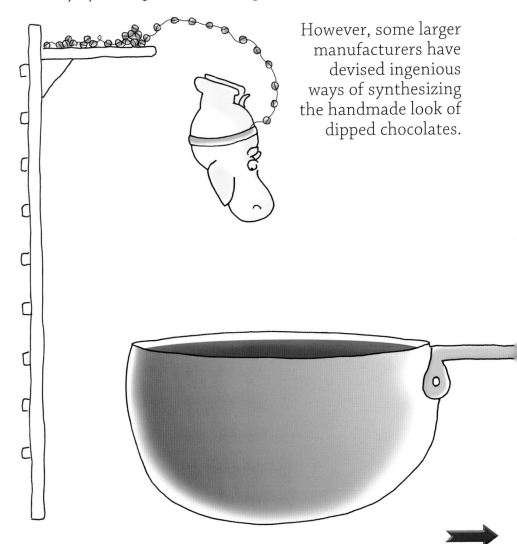

However, some larger manufacturers have devised ingenious ways of synthesizing the handmade look of dipped chocolates.

4. *Shell molding* This is the most complex and sophisticated method of making chocolates. It is by this multi-step technique that most fine "sculptural chocolates" are made—chocolates that masquerade as miniature violins or grape clusters or sailboats or piranhas or what have you.

Here is how shell molding is done:

SHELL PLANT PRODUCTION SEQUENCE

By this method, a chocolatier can make up to five pieces of candy per day. Shell-molded chocolates are priced accordingly.

HOW TO TELL WHAT'S INSIDE

A box of fine chocolates is a glorious object, brimming with possibility and delight. And fear: What if the enticing piece you select turns out to be filled with pineapple mint ketchup gum?

To address this concern, some chocolatiers will mark each piece of candy with a characteristic squiggle or "signature" that whimsically identifies its contents.

For example:

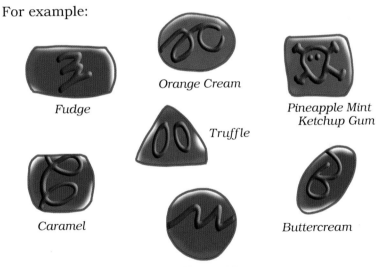

Fudge

Orange Cream

Pineapple Mint Ketchup Gum

Truffle

Caramel

Marshmallow or Marzipan or perhaps Mayonnaise

Buttercream

If you are not experienced at chocolate reading, you can always use the classic method: Stick your finger in the bottom. Put the yucky ones back in the box.

CHOCOLATE PROFILE №5

The Restless Seeker

PERSONALITY	INTROSPECTIVE, IMPATIENT
LIKES	EXPERIENCE
DISLIKES	COMPROMISE
FAVORITE PASTIME	STARGAZING

CHOCOLATE of CHOICE: Craft Chocolate

ULTIMATE CHOCOLATE

The new millennium has brought with it a quiet but insistent counter-trend to mass production: exquisite artisan-made food and drink. Wine, cheese, coffee, beer, bourbon—each has drawn a fanatical core of small-batch makers who strive for new vistas of nuanced taste experience. In turn, those makers attract a core of deeply devoted followers.

And so it is with chocolate.

The chocolate that these driven iconoclasts make is known as "bean to bar" or "craft chocolate." The makers begin at the beginning, working directly with small-scale cacao farmers to determine how to grow and nurture the best possible beans, and how to optimize the methods by which these beans are sorted, fermented, and dried.

Of course, craft chocolate making is not rocket science. It is considerably more difficult than that.

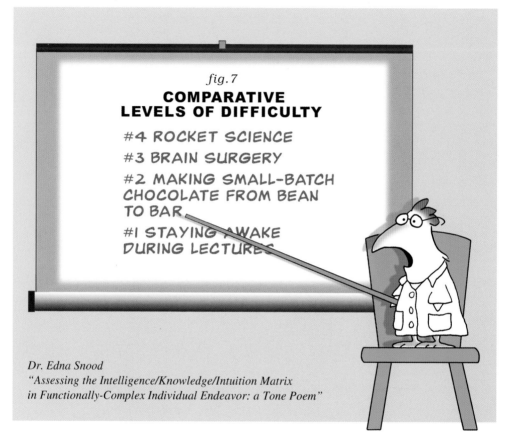

fig. 7

COMPARATIVE LEVELS OF DIFFICULTY

#4 ROCKET SCIENCE

#3 BRAIN SURGERY

#2 MAKING SMALL-BATCH CHOCOLATE FROM BEAN TO BAR

#1 STAYING AWAKE DURING LECTURES

Dr. Edna Snood
"Assessing the Intelligence/Knowledge/Intuition Matrix
in Functionally-Complex Individual Endeavor: a Tone Poem"

It is hard to imagine that anyone has the skill set, not to mention the endurance, to take on this quixotic enterprise. At the very least, a craft chocolate artisan has to be a botanist-explorer-anthropologist-visionary-historian-ethnologist-linguist-sociologist-economist-diplomat-philosopher-accountant-lunatic-negotiator-mechanic-inventor-chemist-designer-packager-merchandiser-promoter.

There may also be sorcery involved.

So what does all this have to do with you? That depends on what you truly want from your chocolate. Sure, you and chocolate have been going along pleasantly, having a lot of fun together. But there may come a time when you are ready to move beyond casual chocolate and commit to something more intense and lasting. This is it.

SEX OR CHOCOLATE: WHICH IS BETTER?

Part Two

THE PHYSIOLOGY AND PSYCHOLOGY OF CHOCOPHILIA

FACT: Chocolate reaches a higher level of consciousness, *in minutes*, than the other leading analgesic.

HERE'S SCIENTIFIC PROOF

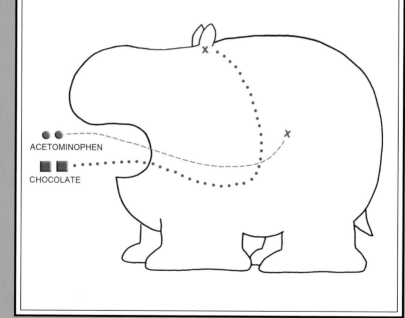

YOUR BODY AND CHOCOLATE

Anything that is greatly admired is bound to be much maligned as well. Chocolate is no exception. There always seems to be someone looking over your shoulder, just waiting for an opportunity to lecture on The Darker Side of Chocolate.

In recent years, the critics have gotten a little quieter, as research scientists have made wondrous discoveries about chocolate's wide-ranging health benefits. Of course, there are a number of us nonscientists who have been vehement all along that chocolate is good for you. Imagine how surprised we are to find out that this is actually true.

And yet the vicious anti-chocolate myths stubbornly persist. What follows are the six most common misconceptions, and the airtight rebuttals.

MYTH Nº 1

"Chocolate is bad for your teeth."

This criticism can be readily dismissed simply by quoting from any of the numerous scientific reports about the proven beneficial effects of cacao on dental health.

"Cocoa bean husk extract is highly effective in reducing *mutans streptococci* counts and plaque deposition when used as a mouth rinse by children."

MYTH № 2

"Chocolate is fattening."

The validity of this claim is extremely unlikely. The average caloric expenditure of managing a personal chocolate supply easily offsets the daily calories of the chocolate itself. Just take a quick glance at this impressive-looking chart that we may or may not have made up off the top of our heads:

ACTIVITY (DAILY)	CALORIES BURNED
THINKING ABOUT CHOCOLATE	295
SHOPPING FOR CHOCOLATE	480
ORGANIZING YOUR CHOCOLATE	743
HIDING ALL OF THE CHOCOLATE BEFORE ANSWERING THE DOOR WHEN COMPANY DROPS BY UNEXPECTEDLY	978

TOTAL EXPENDED CHOCOLATE-RELATED CALORIES: 2,496

**vs. AVERAGE DAILY
CHOCOLATE CALORIES
CONSUMED: 2,305**

MYTH № 3

"Chocolate causes mood instability."

Critics point to the noticeable mood swings of chocolate eaters, fluctuations that are most likely caused by the caffeine and theobromine in cacao. Scientists hypothesize that these stimulants create an artificial "high," soon followed by a marked descent to a "low."

THE STAGES OF CHOCOLATE ASSIMILATION

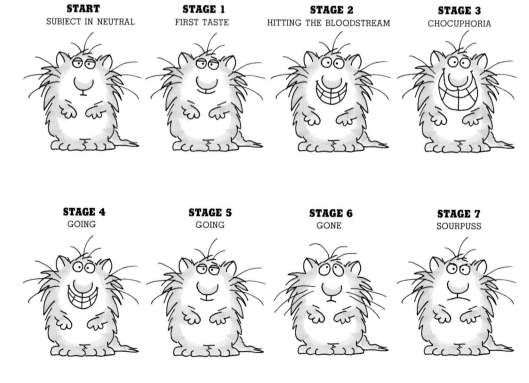

START	STAGE 1	STAGE 2	STAGE 3
SUBJECT IN NEUTRAL	FIRST TASTE	HITTING THE BLOODSTREAM	CHOCUPHORIA

STAGE 4	STAGE 5	STAGE 6	STAGE 7
GOING	GOING	GONE	SOURPUSS

Conceding that there might in fact be something to this, we can nonetheless show that the solution is obvious: To deftly circumvent the undesirable Stages 6 and 7, you need simply to re-introduce chocolate immediately after Stage 5.

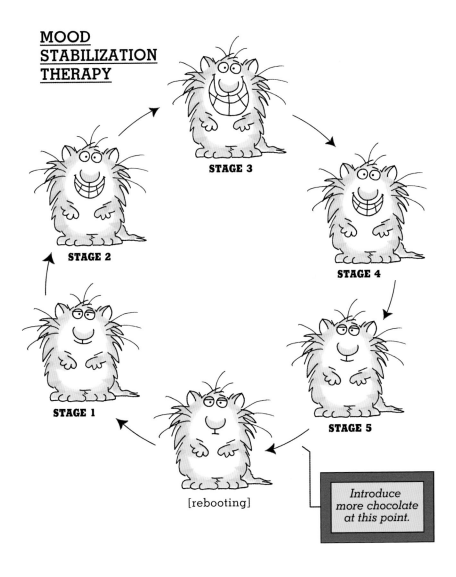

MOOD
STABILIZATION
THERAPY

STAGE 3

STAGE 2

STAGE 4

STAGE 1

STAGE 5

[rebooting]

Introduce
more chocolate
at this point.

MYTH № 4

"Chocolate is nothing more than a substitute for affection."

Much has been made of the scientific finding that cacao has a chemical component—**phenylethylamine**—that is virtually identical to the chemical generated by the brain of an infatuated individual. Careless psychologists have concluded that chocolate obsession must be a form of self-medication for a spurned lover: He or she is looking to synthesize the giddiness of being in love.

As is too often the case with these social scientists, they are taking sound, highly intriguing data and drawing empirically absurd conclusions. What reasonable soul prefers romance to, for example, great chocolate buttercreams?

It would be far more logical to conclude that love is simply a low-quality substitute for chocolate.

MYTH № 5

"Chocolate is bad for your complexion."

This claim is completely without scientific substantiation. In fact, recent research (PICTURED) suggests the exact opposite is the case.

MYTH № 6

"Chocolate is an aphrodisiac."

Okay. Actually, this is true.

AVOIDING NON-CHOCOLATE SITUATIONS

Politely decline all wedding invitations.
Weddings are notorious for white cake
with white icing.

CHOCOLATE AND THE MIND

Chocolate can do wonderful things for your overall sense of well-being. It can offset disappointments, counteract frustrations, provide joy and comfort—even inspire romance.

Yet any serious relationship is not without its trials. Fear of separation gnaws at anyone deeply involved with chocolate. And there ever lurks the dread that your hard-won happiness may be threatened by the unwelcome attentions of others.

If you are truly committed to making your relationship with chocolate a dynamic and satisfying one, you have to be willing to work at it. These are some key guidelines:

1. FIND TIME TO BE ALONE TOGETHER

Chocolate was never meant to be shared.

2. AVOID PROLONGED SEPARATIONS

An extended separation can cause considerable hardship. Make every effort to have your chocolate with you, even if it seems impractical.

3. TAKE TIME TO LISTEN

Pay thoughtful attention. Often chocolate has something to say that only you can hear.

4. MINIMIZE FINANCIAL PRESSURES

If you are experiencing any financial difficulties, chocolate obsession may make them worse. And if trends continue, the economic outlook for chocophiles is bleak.

1930—5¢ bar

2000—99¢ bar

2070 (projected)—
$384.93 bar

But the resourceful chocolatist will not allow money troubles to stand in the way of personal fulfillment. If chocolate cannot be bought, it can still be won by charm.

Or ingenuity.

If you keep in mind the foregoing guidelines, your chocolate-based conflicts will be greatly reduced. Nevertheless, it is important to recognize that no relationship is without its rough patches. There will be times when you and your chocolate are simply not hitting it off.

When this happens, take care to not overreact.

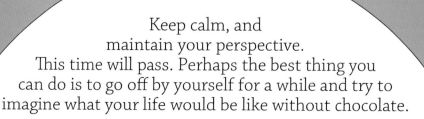

Keep calm, and
maintain your perspective.
This time will pass. Perhaps the best thing you
can do is to go off by yourself for a while and try to
imagine what your life would be like without chocolate.

SOME PROVOCATIVE OBSERVATIONS

The greatest tragedies were written by the Greeks and by Shakespeare. Neither knew chocolate.

The Swiss are noted for peaceful co-existence. They are also known for their lovely chocolate.

THE DEEP QUESTIONS

Much serious thought has been devoted to the formidable subject of chocolate: What does chocolate *mean*? Is the unhindered pursuit of chocolate a right or a privilege? Does the very notion of chocolate preclude the concept of free will?

Yet even these challenging lines of inquiry seemed to blur when the **Irritating Skeptical Rationalists** first posed that profound and unsettling question:

How do we know that chocolate exists?

This had everyone stumped (and not a little depressed) for quite some time.

Then the **Empirical Condescensionists** came along and pointed out that what we mean by "knowing" is "that which we learn through our senses." For example, we *know* that chocolate exists because we can *taste* it. (Although of course it then ceases to exist pretty quickly.)

Challenging both groups to go further, the **Theosophical Gastronomes** posed the radical question: Assuming that chocolate exists, does that *ipso facto* verify the existence of a Supreme Bean?

It was the **Untroubled Capitalists** who first realized that it doesn't really matter whether chocolate exists or not, as long as people buy it.

IS THE CHOCOLATE AT ITS BEST?

As with most fine things, chocolate has its season. There is a simple memory aid that you can use to determine whether it is the correct time to order chocolate dishes:

ANY MONTH WHOSE NAME CONTAINS THE LETTER A, E, OR U IS THE PROPER TIME FOR CHOCOLATE

Part Three

KNOWING YOUR CHOCOLATE

In taste tests conducted nationwide,
chocolate lovers were
blindfolded and asked to compare
five different premium chocolate creams.

The result?

3 OUT OF 4 PANELISTS
ACTUALLY RESENTED
HAVING BEEN BLINDFOLDED

EVALUATING CHOCOLATE

Chocolate experts judge the quality of chocolate by these four basic criteria:

★ *Presentation*

This means how the chocolate looks. The chocolate should have an even, glossy surface. Lack of shine indicates staleness and/or questionable moral character.

★ *Snap*

This term refers to the way the chocolate performs under pressure. Good chocolate should have a lively, decisive break. If it splinters, it is too dry. If it breaks reluctantly, it is too waxy. If it folds, something is definitely wrong.

★ *Mouth Feel*

This somewhat unpoetic expression basically means texture. The "mouth feel" of chocolate (dry/gritty, moist/smooth) depends mostly on how long the chocolate has been **conched**, i.e., made smooth by slopping around in shell-shaped vats. Chocolate that wears away more than twenty percent of your tongue has not been conched long enough.

Note: Judging the texture of chocolate by "hand feel" is not widely recommended.

★ *Taste*

This is the term used by wily experts to mean "taste." The three primary components of chocolate taste are **sweetness** (due to percentage of sugar), **chocolateyness** (due to percentage of cocoa solids), and **bouquet** (due to source of the beans, the specifics of the processing, and the self-importance of the taster).

Sometimes the experience of chocolate is affected most of all by yet another factor:

★ *Price*

A "high price" tends to enhance the delight in **received** chocolate, yet compromise the enjoyment of **bought** chocolate.

Using the above criteria, a panel of experts will generally agree on the character of a given bar. Yet, curiously, there will rarely be any consensus on the quality of that exact same chocolate.

Q: HOW WOULD YOU DESCRIBE GZÖRNENBLATT'S SEMI-FAMOUS CHOCOLATE SLAB?

"Noble presentation, hearty snap, chalky mouth feel. Taste is acidic, somewhat chocolatey, with a husky bouquet (notes of cinnamon, cardboard). Faintly presumptuous price."

Q: ON A SCALE OF 1 TO 10, HOW WOULD YOU RATE GZÖRNENBLATT'S SEMI-FAMOUS CHOCOLATE SLAB?

But when all is said and done—and quite a lot of it eaten—truly the most important thing is this: You like what you like. Chocolate beauty is in the eye of the beholder. In the nose of the be-smeller. Mouth of the be-taster. Whatever. Go for it.

LOWERING THE BAR

If the go-to chocolate candy bar of your childhood no longer has the same appeal for you, it might not be because your tastes have changed. More likely, the candy bar itself has changed.

With most popular chocolate candy bars, the name and wrapper have stayed pretty much the same for the better part of a century. But over time, many of these bars have seen a gradual reduction of their true chocolate ingredients, with some synthetic things quietly replacing the real ones.

LOT #7695-K3
"GOOD" UNTIL
NOV 3 2078

INGREDIENTS: INVERT SYRUP #26-C; INDESTRUCTIBLE® MILK; ALKALIZED COCOA-LIKE POWDERY STUFF; PLAS-TIC; PRETEND COCOA BUTTER; BHA; BHT; MSG; TBHQ; PGPR; OMG; WTH?!

Nutrition Fa
Serving Size 1 bar
Servings Per Container 1

Amount Per Serving
Calories 473   Calories from

% Daily Va
Total Fat 19 g / Sat.Fat 12 g
Sodium 68 mg
Total Carbohydrate 51 g
Protein 5 g
Experiential Value trace   1%

Vitamin A .3% • Vitamin C 1% • Calcium 5% • Iron 2%
Not a significant source of actual chocolate.
*Percent Daily Values are based on a 2,000 calorie diet.

For the real taste you remember, don't buy candy that says "chocolatey" instead of "chocolate." And avoid mystery ingredients. They will only break your heart.

Dr. Merton Calypso, Ph.G.

HOW TO STORE YOUR CHOCOLATE

Chocolate lasts longest if kept in a
cool, dry, airtight container.

HANDLING CHOCOLATE

Chocolate is quite temperamental, and requires cautious handling. You can minimize the frustrations of chocolate care by becoming familiar with its standard patterns of behavior.

If stored at cold temperatures (below 55°F) chocolate **sweats** when brought too quickly to room temperature.

At warm temperatures (above 85°F) chocolate may **bloom**: The cocoa butter rises to the surface and produces a rough, whitish film.

At warmer temperatures (90°F to 220°F) chocolate **melts**.

At high temperatures (above 220°F) chocolate **burns**.

In the heat of commerce, chocolate ***conglomerates***.

At first, you are not likely to realize when a chocolate brand that you like and admire has conglomerated, since the brand name and packaging will be unchanged. But over time, the quality may steadily ratchet down. Historically, conglomeration has not often been kind to chocolate.

KEEPING YOUR CHOCOLATE FRESH

Chocolate is not only sensitive to temperature, but to its social environment as well. If chocolate associates too freely with influential foods, its taste will inevitably be compromised.

Because of the impressionable nature of chocolate, it is advisable not to store it in your refrigerator. For shorter-term storage, a cool and dry cupboard is best. For longer keeping, wrap the chocolate well and hide it in your freezer.

The most conscientious among us will see to it that storage is really not an issue.

HOW TO MAKE CHOCOLATE STAINS DISAPPEAR

REMOVAL OF CHOCOLATE FROM POROUS MATERIAL

1. Scrape off excess chocolate
   with your fingernail.
   (In polite society, use a
   demitasse spoon.)

2. Apply cornstarch, to absorb oils.

3. Apply cleaning fluid. Let dry.

4. Wet fabric, and apply an enzyme paste.
   Let stand 2 hours.

5. Remove the paste using a cleaning spatula, assuming there actually is such a thing.

6. Wash the fabric with water and detergent.

IF STAIN PERSISTS

7. Apply a few drops of ammonia. Wait 7 minutes.

8. Neutralize the ammonia with a few drops of vinegar.

9. Wash the fabric again. The stain— and perhaps the place where it was— will be gone.

ALTERNATE METHOD

ALTERNATE METHOD

1. Melt 2 pounds of chocolate for each pound of fabric.

2. Thoroughly immerse the fabric in the liquid chocolate and let stand.

3. Rinse well.

REMOVAL OF CHOCOLATE FROM NON-POROUS MATERIAL

These spots are easily licked.

BEING PREPARED

If the remotest possibility exists that you could become snowbound, take this commonsense precaution:

1. REMOVE AND DISCARD ALL OF THE INSULATION FROM YOUR SKI JACKET.

2. REPLACE WITH 7 POUNDS SHAVED CHOCOLATE.

3. RESEW SEAMS.

WARNING: NEVER WARM UP IN FRONT OF A HEAT SOURCE WITHOUT FIRST REMOVING THE JACKET.

Making your own chocolate at home is
a little extra work, but well worth it.

Part Four

WHERE TO GET IT

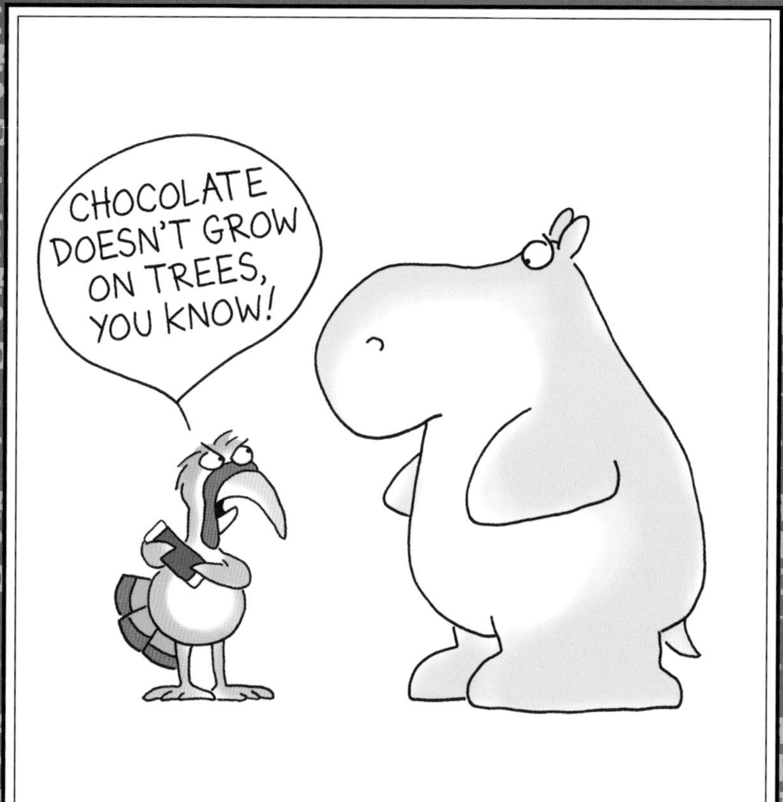
CHOCOLATE DOESN'T GROW ON TREES, YOU KNOW!

GROWING YOUR OWN CHOCOLATE

In these uncertain times, self-sufficiency makes good sense. With that in mind, perhaps you might consider producing your own personal supply of chocolate. Here's how:

STEP 1: GROW THE BEANS

YOU WILL NEED

- *1 smallish plantation*
- *4,000 cacao seedlings*
- *a shovel*

Instructions:

1. Move to within 20° N or S of the Equator (on dry land).

2. For each 5 pounds of chocolate desired per year, plant 1 cacao seedling, locating each in the shade of a larger tree (banana, mango, etc.). Place at a density of approximately 1,000 trees per hectare.

3. Wait 5 to 7 years for the cacao trees to mature.

You are now ready to harvest.

STEP 2: HARVEST THE BEANS

YOU WILL NEED

- *1 pole knife*
- *1 machete*
- *390 fermenting trays*

Instructions:

1. Using your pole knife, carefully gather all ripe pods. **DO NOT CLIMB THE TREES.**

2. Gently split the pods open with the machete. Scoop out the beans.

3. Place the beans in trays in a draft-free area, and cover with burlap. Let stand until the beans have turned medium-brown (about 1 week).

4. Dry the beans in the sun, stirring occasionally until their moisture content is below 7% (about 3 days).

You are now ready to make chocolate.

STEP 3: MAKE THE CHOCOLATE LIQUOR

YOU WILL NEED

- *1 cleaning machine*
- *1 scale*
- *1 roaster*
- *1 cracker and fanner*
- *1 grinding mill*

Instructions:

1. Pass the beans through your cleaning machine to remove dried pulp and other extraneous matter.

2. Weigh and sort the beans.

3. Roast the beans at 250°F for 2 hours.

4. Use your cracker and fanner to remove the shells from the beans, leaving the nibs.

5. Crush the nibs in your grinding mill. The heat generated will liquefy the pulp, creating your "chocolate liquor."

**You now have the base
raw material of all
chocolate bars and creations.**

STEP 4: FINESSING THE FLAVOR AND TEXTURE

YOU WILL NEED

• *the chocolate liquor you made*
• *sugar*
• *an industrial conching machine*

Instructions:

1. Slowly bring the chocolate liquor to 120°F, stirring gently.

2. Add the sugar, then put the mixture into your conching machine.

3. Conch for anywhere between 8 and 35 hours, testing every hour until both the taste and texture please you. (Or you can test it every 5 minutes just for the heck of it.)

YOU DID IT!
You made chocolate!

TEMPERING CHOCOLATE

Before you can turn fabulous chocolate into fabulous bars and/or fabulous chocolate-covered things, you will first need to **temper** the chocolate. Tempering is what gives chocolate its smooth, glossy finish and its lively snap.

If you have ever tried to make chocolates simply by dipping the centers in melted chocolate, you have seen vividly why tempering is so important.

WELL—TEMPERED
CHOCOLATE

BAD—TEMPERED
CHOCOLATE

What you are looking to do is generate abundant beta crystals, in order to stratify the cocoa fat. To accomplish this, all you will need is a marble slab, an angled spatula, a chocolate thermometer, the proper humidity conditions, a devil-may-care attitude, and an advanced degree in molecular chemistry from an accredited major university.

Dreams reveal the soul.

SHOPPING FOR CHOCOLATE

GROCERY STORES

Freshness, variety, and low low prices: three good reasons to avoid buying chocolate at grocery stores. These stores rob chocolate-buying of all its romance. The low prices deprive you of that vital sense of sacrifice and suffering. The sheer abundance makes your purchase appear trivial. The relentless freshness tells you that many others have been here before you, and this can make your own precious relationship with chocolate seem tawdry and cheap.

6

CANDY
CHOCOLATE
BAKING NEEDS

DEPARTMENT STORES

Many of the tonier department stores now devote entire sections to chocolate, featuring a range of uncommon bars, imported boxed chocolates, and regional chocolate specialties. Invariably, the chocolate department goes by a sophisticated French name, such as "Le Chocolatier" or "Au Chocolat" or "Le Bon Bon-Bon."

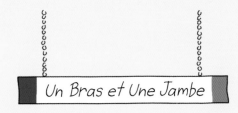

The reason for the proliferation of chocolate departments is simple: Shrewd store merchandisers know that an unusual, high-quality chocolate section will bring in traffic.

Wherever store management recognizes the importance of its chocolate department, you are assured of finding rare, exquisite confectionery. But you will definitely pay through the snout for it.

CHOCOLATE SHOPS

"Chocolate Shop" is a catch-all term for small retailers of made-on-the-premises confectionery. These shops thrive by offering fresh and unusual chocolate creations.

In nearly all cases, the products "made" by a Chocolate Shop are only molded by them, using chocolate that they buy in bulk from a large manufacturer. The machinery for making chocolate is very elaborate, and taking on this aspect of production is beyond the reach of most chocolatiers.

What these Chocolate Shops do make is **chocolates**: They create their own special centers, and then dip them by hand in their sourced chocolate couverture. The taste and texture of that couverture matters greatly, of course, but it is the uniqueness of the proprietary centers that makes a shop truly unforgettable.

There is a great mystique about "hand-dipped chocolates." To many connoisseurs, this phrase connotes quality, care, and craftsmanship. But when you come right down to it, hand-dipping is not necessarily the wonderful process you imagine it to be.

DRUGSTORES

In an emergency, look for a drugstore. They are often open when other stores are closed, and they do sell over-the-counter chocolate.

Be aware, though, that since they have a virtual monopoly on off-hour chocolate, pharmacies tend to be somewhat blasé about freshness.

CHOCOLATE BY MAIL

If you have no ready access to fine chocolate, you might try remote ordering. Whether through mail-order catalogs or online, you can find extraordinary things that can be delivered right to your mailbox. The only real disadvantage is that your timing has to be near-perfect. The chocolate may arrive late,

or you may arrive late,

or a neighbor
might arrive
right on time.

Perhaps you dream of building your ideal home.

Part Five

MAKING THINGS WITH CHOCOLATE

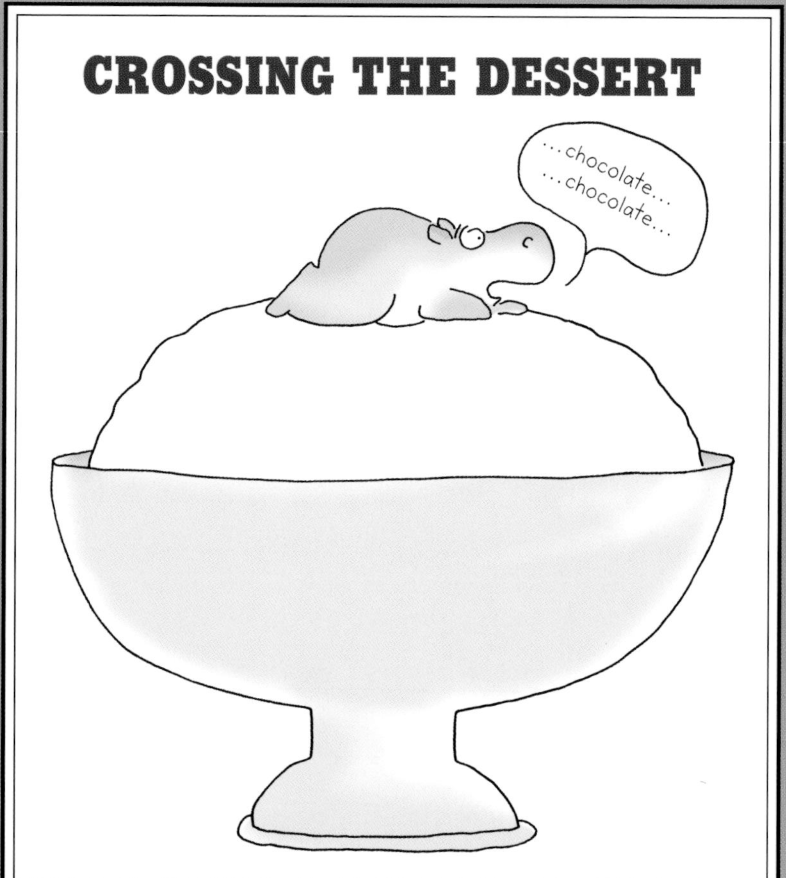
CROSSING THE DESSERT
...chocolate...
...chocolate...

CHOCOLATE COOKERY

Chocolate cookery would seem to be the perfect pastime for those devoted to chocolate. Unfortunately, this is not really the case. Chocolate enthusiasts are not known for their patience.

Though it is true that books of terrific chocolate recipes tend to sell quite well, these cookbooks are generally bought not by chocolate lovers themselves, but by their well-meaning friends.

Think about it: Would any true chocolate devotee, deciding to spend good money for something rectangular and deeply satisfying, buy a *book*?

The recipes that follow take a low frustration tolerance into account. Nearly all of them are short but sweet.

RECIPES ➤

NOTES ON MELTING CHOCOLATE

In any recipe calling for liquefied chocolate, care must be taken to melt the chocolate gradually.

Milk chocolate requires even lower temperatures.

Do not allow any moisture whatsoever to combine with the chocolate while you are melting it. A single drop may cause the mixture to suddenly stiffen or "seize."

BROWNIES

Yield: Immediately (makes 24)

Preheat oven to 350°F.
In the top of a double boiler, melt together, then let cool:

6 ounces unsweetened chocolate
½ cup unsalted butter

In a large bowl, beat well:

3 eggs

Add gradually to eggs, and beat until foamy:

¾ cup white sugar
1 cup light brown sugar
2 teaspoons vanilla extract

Gently fold the cooled chocolate mixture into the
egg mixture, then add:

1¼ cups all-purpose flour

Add:

1 tablespoon coconut oil

Bake in a greased 9 x 13-inch pan for approximately 25 minutes.

TESTING FOR DONENESS:
The brownies are done
when an inserted fork
comes out clean.

HIPPO POT de MOUSSE

Makes 6 individual portions

In the top of a double boiler, melt:

4 ounces semisweet chocolate
2 ounces unsweetened chocolate

Let the chocolate cool for 5 minutes.
Meanwhile, whip together until stiff:

1 pint heavy cream, well chilled
1 teaspoon almond extract

Gently fold the cooled chocolate into the whipped cream.
(There will be many small flecks of chocolate in the mixture.)

Spoon the dessert into 6 large wine glasses. Chill 1 hour.
Garnish with fresh berries.

SERVES 1

CHOCOLATE CHIP COOKIE

Theoretical yield: 36 cookies

Preheat oven to 375°F.
Cream together until light and fluffy:

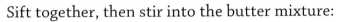

¾ cup unsalted butter
¾ cup light brown sugar
¼ cup dark brown sugar

Beat in:

1 egg
1 teaspoon vanilla extract

Sift together, then stir into the butter mixture:

1⅓ cups all-purpose flour
¾ teaspoon baking soda

Chop into pieces, then stir in:

2 bittersweet chocolate bars (3.5 ounces each)

It is customary at this point
to sample the batter.

Drop the remaining batter from a teaspoon onto a greased
cookie sheet. Bake the cookie about 10 minutes.

MOLDING CHOCOLATE RABBITS

Have ready (clean and dry):

10 metal or ceramic bunny-shaped molds

Over hot water or low flame, melt to 90°F:

5 pounds professional-quality couverture

Pour the chocolate into the molds. Tap them gently on a hard surface, to release air bubbles. Place molds in a freezer until firm (about 10 minutes). Invert to unmold.

OLD-WORLD ARTISANAL METHOD

Stand on end:

1 block of chocolate, 5 x 5 x 9 feet

Using a mallet and chisel, chip away all pieces that do not contribute meaningfully to an overall impression of rabbititity.

CHOCOLATE SOUFFLÉ

Makes 6 individual portions

Preheat oven to 375°F. Butter 6 small ramekins, and coat them with white sugar. In the top of a double boiler, melt:

8 ounces bittersweet chocolate
5 tablespoons unsalted butter

Remove from heat, and stir in:

1 teaspoon vanilla extract

In a separate bowl, beat until frothy:

6 large egg yolks
2 tablespoons water
2 teaspoons fresh lime juice

Slowly add:

2 tablespoons white sugar

Beat on high for 2 minutes. Fold into the chocolate mixture. In a separate bowl, beat until frothy:

6 large egg whites

Slowly add, and continue beating until the whites hold a stiff peak:

½ cup white sugar
½ teaspoon sea salt

Fold the egg white mixture into the chocolate mixture until just blended. Spoon into the ramekins. Place the soufflés on a baking sheet, and bake for 18 minutes. Remove from oven, and dust with **confectioners' sugar**. Serve sooner than immediately.

PLEASE NOTE: Soufflés are very moody. Do not open the oven during baking. Serve the soufflé promptly, and keep it away from drafts.

chocolate soufflé    *chocolate souffloppe*

SALVAGING FAILED DESSERTS

If your chocolate dessert doesn't turn out, don't panic. You have two great options for making the best of a bad situation:

1. You can hope no one notices.

2. You can cleverly repurpose the dessert. For instance:

- Unsuccessful fudge makes an excellent ice cream topping.
- Unsuccessful brownies make a delicious pudding.
- An unsuccessful soufflé makes a rakish beret.

INTERNATIONAL CHOCOLATE PHRASEBOOK

INTERNATIONAL CHOCOLATE PHRASEBOOK

When traveling abroad, the quickest and most reliable way to locate chocolate is to ask around:

> ## "Excuse me,
> ## where is the nearest chocolate?"

AUSTRIA, GERMANY

"Entschuldigen Sie bitte, wo ist die nächste Schokolade?"
(Ent-SHOOL-dee-gen zee BIT-tuh, VŌ ist dee NEX-tuh shō-cō-LAH-duh?)

BELGIUM, CANADA (Québec), FRANCE

"Excusez-moi, où est le chocolat le plus proche?"
(Ex-COO-zay mwah, oo eh luh shō-cō-LAH l'ploo prōsh?)

CHINA

"对不起，这里是最近的巧克力？"

(DAY-boo-chee, ZHAY-lee shee zwee-jeen deh chock-a-LEE?)

ENGLAND

"I say, beg pardon, Old Man, but could you direct me to a nearby purveyor of chocolate, eh what?"

(AH-ee SEH-ee, behg PAH-dun, uhld maan, baht cood ee-OO die-REKT mee too eh NEE-ah-BAH-ee puh-VAY-aw ruv CHUCK-uh-lit, eh hwutt?)

ITALY

"Mi scusi, dov'è il cioccolato più vicino?"

(Mee SKOO-zee, DŌ-vay eel chō-cō-LAH-tō PEE-oo vee-CHEE-nō?)

"Excuse me, where is the nearest chocolate?"

JAPAN

"すみません、最寄りのチョコレートはどこですか？"
(Soo-mee-mah-sen, mō-yō-ree nō chō-kō-reh-tō wah dō-kō dehs kah?)

MEXICO, SPAIN

"Por favor, ¿dónde está el chocolate más cercana?"
(POOR fah-VOOR, DŌN-day ess-TAH el shō-cō-LAH-tay MAHS sayr-KAH-nah?)

MIDDLE EARTH, NEW ZEALAND

"ᚦᛣᚺᚿᚲᚻ, ᛩᛝᚺᛏᚻ ᛁᚲ ᚠᛝᚨᚤᚨᛣᚿᛏᚻᛉ"
(PLEEZ, oo-AIR iz CHOCK-lit?)

QO'NOS (Klingon Planet)

"⟨Klingon script⟩?"
(Nook-dock YOOCH dah-PULL?)

ROMAN EMPIRE

"Ardonpay emay, erewhay isyay ethay earestnay ocolatechay?
(AR-dun-pay EE-may, AIR-way IZ-yay UH-thay EER-ist-nay OCK-lit-chay?)

(Caesar Hogustus)

RUSSIA

"Извините, где находится ближайший шоколад?"
(Iz-vih-NEE-tyeh, g-DYEH nuh-KHŌ-jits-yuh blih-ZHAI-shee shuh-kuh-LAHT?

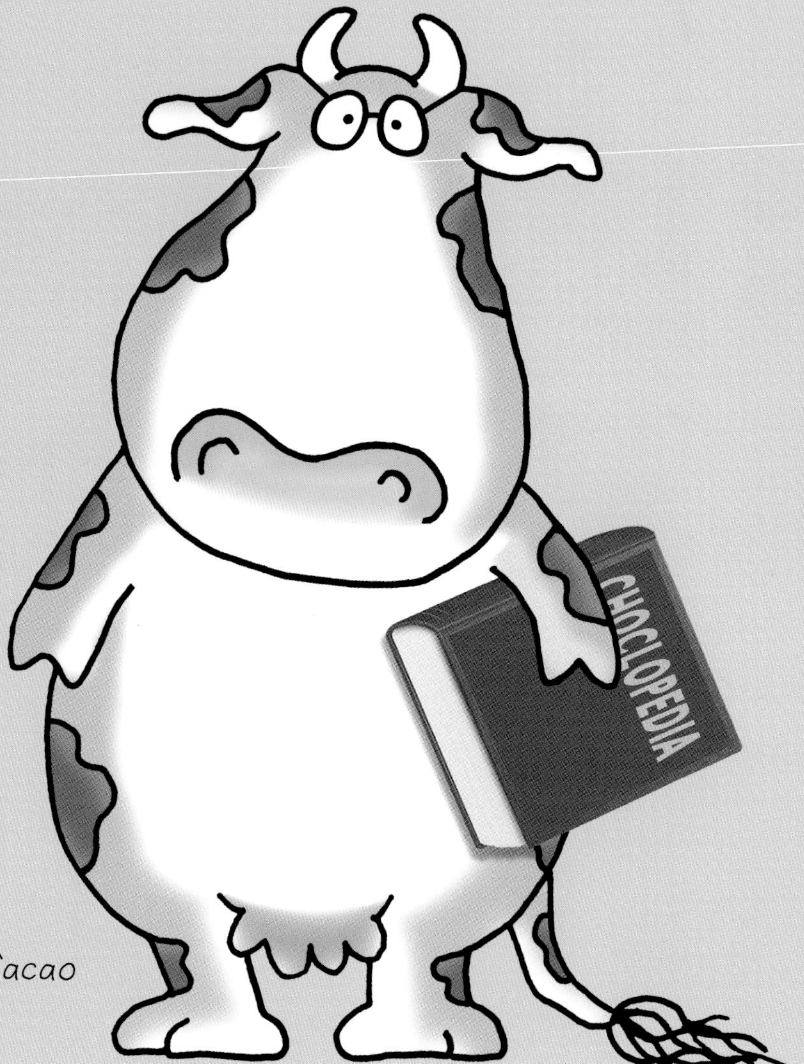
CHOCLOPEDIA

Cacao

A GLOSSARY OF TERMS

CACAO
1. Beanlike seeds from which chocolate is made. (Also called COCOA BEANS.)
2. Small tropical American evergreen tree that bears the pods containing the beans.
3. The product resulting from processing the beans, i.e., cocoa and cocoa butter.
4. That thing that goes Moo.

CHOCOLATE
A mystical elixir of unparalleled healing power and infinite nuance. Great on ice cream.

CHOCOPHILIA
Chocolate obsession.
(from the Ancient Greek χοκοπίλια, which literally translates as "How come we have a word for this when we Europeans will not actually know about chocolate for another two thousand years?")

MISER
Someone who won't share his/her chocolate with you.

MOOCH
Someone who expects you to share your chocolate with him/her.

THANK YOU

for your steadfast friendship
and skillful guidance.
If there were ever people
I would share my chocolate with,
it would definitely
be you guys.

SUZANNE RAFER
(my trusty editor)
AND

BOB ALESSI
SUZIE BOLOTIN
DARCY BOYNTON
KEITH BOYNTON
LAURIE BOYNTON & CARL YEICH
PAM BOYNTON & JOHN STEY
BOYNTONS & RADERS & STEYS
HELEN BRANDT
THE CAPECELATROS
THE CLARKES
MATT COLLINS
ROBIN COREY
MARC DITTMER
PAGE EDMUNDS
LINDA JEANNE EPSTEIN & FAMILY
MIKE & BETH FORD
LUCY FRISCH
SARAH GETZ
MERYL & DON GUMMER
MIKE HAGERMAN
PAUL HANSON
NOREEN HERITS
KIM HICKS
MIKE & LINDY KEISER
THE KIRBERS
EDITE KROLL & KEITH WALKER
THE LINNEY/SCHAUER FAMILY

RANDALL LOTOWICZ
PETER LUNDEEN
TIM JONES MALLOY
JENNY MANDEL
THE MANNS
CAITLIN McEWAN
DEVIN McEWAN
McEWANS & MARKOFFS
SELINA MEERE
THEO MENEAU
KELLEY MERWIN
TERRY ORTOLANI & FAMILY
ANNE PICHON &
YOSHINORI TANUMA
NORA & BOB RIVKIN
DAVID SCHILLER
ALINDA & BEVAN STANLEY
GRAHAM STONE
CHERYL SWIFT
MIKE VAGO
WICK WALKER
WALTER WEINTZ
CAROL WHITE
JESSICA WIENER
DOUG WOLFF
CAROLAN WORKMAN
THE YANKOVICS

THANK YOU

for the inspiring work you do.
You indeed make the world
a better place.

AMEDEI
ASKINOSIE
BERNACHON
COPPENEUR
DANDELION CHOCOLATE
DAN'S CHOCOLATES
DICK TAYLOR
E. GUITTARD
FRENCH BROAD CHOCOLATE
HARBOR SWEETS
JACQUES TORRES CHOCOLATE
JOHN KELLY CHOCOLATES
KEE'S CHOCOLATES
LI-LAC CHOCOLATES
MARIEBELLE, NEW YORK
MICHEL CLUIZEL
Alan McClure/PATRIC CHOCOLATE
Kathy Wiley/POCO DOLCE CHOCOLATE
RECCHIUTI CONFECTIONS
RICHARD DONNELLY FINE CHOCOLATES
Chantal Coady/ROCOCO CHOCOLATES
Colin Gasko/ROGUE CHOCOLATIER
Kathleen King/TATE'S BAKE SHOP
Katrina Markoff/VOSGES HAUT-CHOCOLAT
WILLIE'S CACAO

Matthew Rubiner/RUBINER'S, Great Barrington, Massachusetts
Michael Bortz/CITY BAKERY, Denver, Colorado
CHOCOSPHERE
COCOA RUNNERS
THE MEADOW, New York City
THE PANTRY, Washington Depot, Connecticut
David Lebovitz

WIKIPEDIA

It's so hard to say goodbye.

CHOCOLATE!

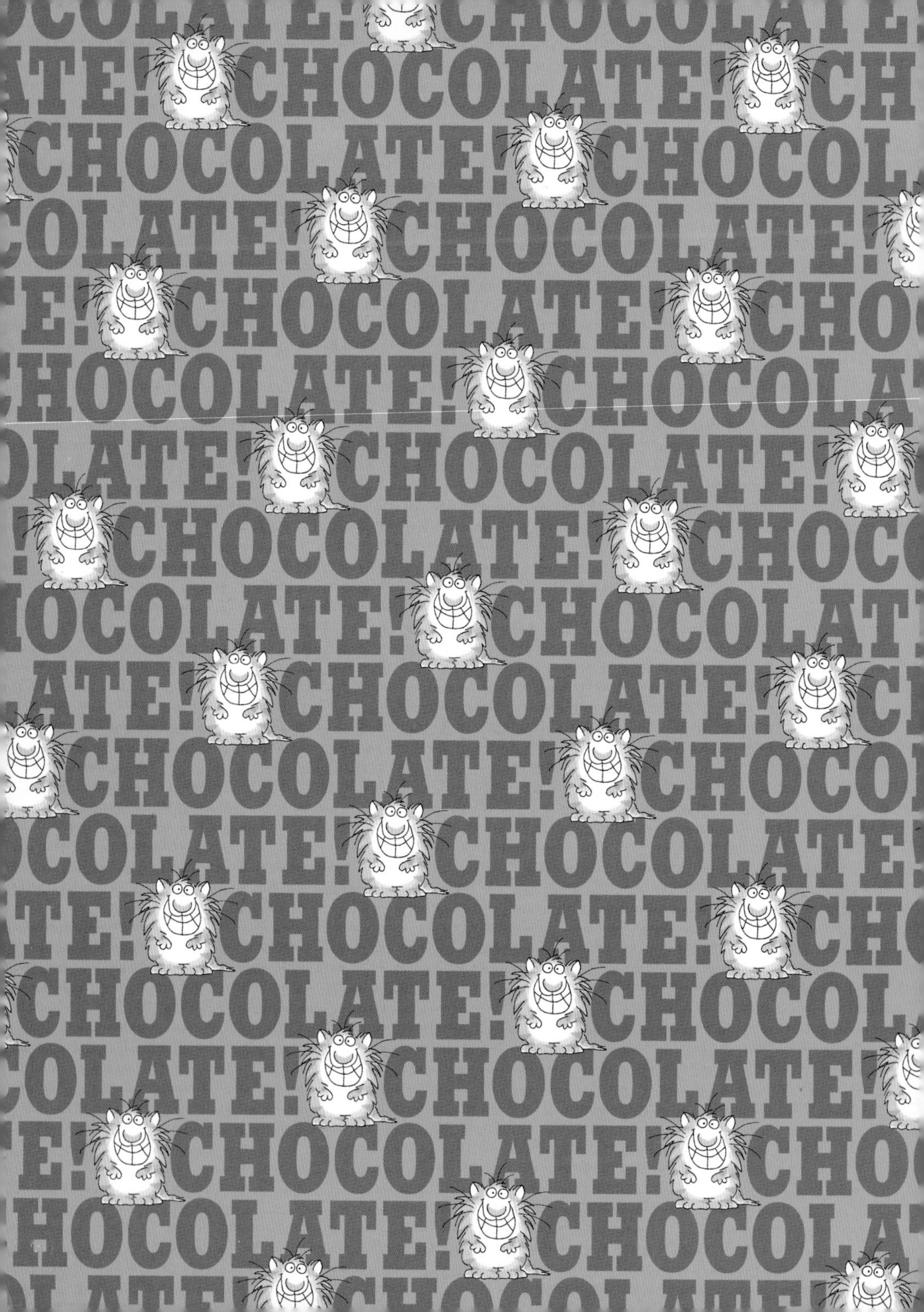
CHOCOLATE!